GALMART ESL MANGA #1:
ARGUMENTATIVE ESSAYS
(A READER FOR INTERMEDIATE ELLS)

BY LIA MARTYNOVA
AND BOB GAULKE

ART BY ELVIS GONZALES
EDITED BY REGINALD THOMAS

Designed by Jenn Lawrence

Cover illustration and all interior illustrations by Elvis Gonzales

Special thanks to Megan Kennelly, Jill Shimmel Sopa, Stacy Falberg, Dan Gieck, Mike Mena, & Rebecca Akselrad for their invaluable feedback and guidance.

Intermediate-level English Language Learners (ELLs) are challenged to find source material in their efforts to write persuasive or argumentative essays as they must as part of the Common Core State Standards. To this end, GalMart has adapted recent stories of interest to teenagers and have illustrated them in a contemporary manga style.

In this first volume, students will find facts and data to support both sides of some of the most current questions of debate, along with comprehension check exercises, and New York State English Language Arts -modelled multiple choice questions.

We realize that students will be receiving adequate guidance in the essay drafting process, but hope that our illustrated content will be of service in supporting the shaping of arguments of your students.

LIA MARTYNOVA
BOB GAULKE

TABLE OF CONTENTS

ARGUMENT WRITING SAMPLE ESSAY

Winning the Lottery Is a Good Idea

INTRODUCTION

The question before us is whether winning the lottery changes your life for the better or for the worse. **The controversy over this issue affects** everyone who plays the lottery. Ninety percent of people play the lottery, and all hope to win. **Those in favor** of playing the lottery say that winning the lottery changes your life for the better. **Those opposed** to playing the lottery **counter** that winning the lottery may change your life for the worse. **Both sides give interesting viewpoints about** winning the lottery. **However, in the second** comic the arguments are **exaggerated**. In the first comic that is in favor of the lottery, the arguments are more **persuasive**. **Consequently, I conclude** that winning the lottery changes your life for the better.

THESIS (CLAIM)

BODY PARAGRAPHS

CLAIM PARAGRAPHS

REASON 1 - TOPIC SENTENCE

If you win the lottery, you could be rich for the rest of your life. **For example**, Maribel Torres won $100 million. She hired financial advisers to help her manage her money. She put $45 million in bonds and $35 million in oil and real estate. In 10 years, she planned to have 10 times more money.

EVIDENCE 1

REASON 2 - TOPIC SENTENCE

You can use your money to help others. **For example**, Phil Struck, a junior high school teacher, got $80 million from Powerball in 1997. He bought 226 acres of land in Alabama and opened a camp for kids. He also works as a volunteer basketball coach and drives his old Jeep.

EVIDENCE 2

REASON 3 - TOPIC SENTENCE

Some people go up in social status and become bosses. **For example**, Muhit Hasan worked at McDonald's for 26 years flipping hamburgers. In 2008, he bought a Sandwich franchise and became the owner and manager. Muhit Hasan was a worker and after winning the lottery he became the boss. He still has the same friends as before.

EVIDENCE 3

COUNTER-CLAIM

Some opponents of playing the lottery talk about tragedies such as when people have been killed over the money or when they lose their house in fire. Some lottery winners spend their money quickly and become poorer than they were before or their families break up because of the money. **Although this may be true**, the majority of lottery winners live better lives.

COUNTER-CLAIM EVIDENCE

CONCLUSION

In conclusion, I believe that winning the lottery changes your life for the better. **Surely** there are people who don't know how to manage their money, and they get in trouble. **However**, many lottery winners manage their money well and benefit from their winnings.

In bold → TRANSITION WORDS AND WORDS THAT HELP TO STRUCTURE AN ARGUMENT.

REAL LIFE STORIES

LOTTERY WINNERS COULD BE RICH FOR THE REST OF THEIR LIVES.

EXCITED

WHOO-HOO!!! I'M A MILLIONAIRE!

WINNING NUMBERS ARE 53, 66, 25...

WINNER
53 66 25 11

MARIBEL TORRES WON A $100 MILLION POWERBALL JACKPOT.

HEY GUYS, MANAGE MY MONEY WELL!

CONFIDENT

WE WILL INVEST $45 MILLION IN BONDS, AND $35 MILLION IN OIL AND REAL ESTATE. IN 10 YEARS, YOU WILL HAVE 10 TIMES MORE.

SHE HIRED FINANCIAL ADVISERS TO HELP HER MANAGE HER MONEY.

LOTTERY WINNERS COULD SPEND MONEY TO HELP OTHERS.

SURPRISED

TONIGHT'S WINNING NUMBERS ARE 80, 84, 14...

OH MY GOD I'M RICH!!!

WITH THAT MONEY, HE BOUGHT 226 ACRES OF LAND IN ALABAMA AND OPENED A CAMP FOR KIDS. HE ALSO WORKS AS A VOLUNTEER BASKETBALL COACH AND DRIVES HIS OLD JEEP.

I BOUGHT THIS CAMP FOR YOU...

GENEROUS

THANKS, COACH.

LOTTERY WINNERS CAN BECOME BOSSES.

NO WAY! I DON'T BELIEVE IT!

SHOCKED

64 60

DINER

IN 2008, HE BOUGHT A SANDWICH FRANCHISE AND BECAME THE OWNER AND MANAGER. HE STILL HAS THE SAME FRIENDS AS BEFORE.

SATISFIED

NOW I'M THE BOSS!

Muhit Hasan
$187,000,000.00

SAY WHAT?

FILL IN THE BLANKS USING THE ADJECTIVES BELOW

CONFIDENT	SATISFIED
EXCITED	SHOCKED
GENEROUS	SURPRISED

Panel 1:

I'M SO HAPPY THE PRINCIPAL CALLED MY NAME. I'M SO _____ TO BE GOING ON THE FIELD TRIP.

I AM _____ THAT JEREMY IS ALSO GOING ON THE FIELD TRIP. HE IS IN DETENTION A LOT.

Panel 2:

WOW, EMMA YOU ARE NOT SHY. YOU WALKED UP TO ANTHONY AND ASKED HIM TO THE DANCE.

MILEY CYRUS IS NOT AFRAID TO ASK A BOY TO THE DANCE. I WANT TO BE _____ LIKE HER.

Panel 3:

BILL GATES GAVE GREEN PARK JUNIOR HIGH MONEY TO BUY EVERY STUDENT A LAPTOP.

WE MUST WRITE HIM A THANK YOU EMAIL FOR HIS _____ GIFT.

Panel 4:

DID YOU HEAR NEWS ABOUT DARRELL'S OLDER BROTHER? HE WAS KILLED IN A CAR CRASH.

HE WAS SUCH A GOOD BASKETBALL PLAYER.

I WAS _____. EVERYBODY SAID HE WAS A VERY GOOD DRIVER.

Panel 5:

JULIAN AND GRACE WORKED ALL NIGHT ON THEIR WORLD WAR II PROJECT. IT WAS VERY WELL DONE.

THEY WERE _____ WITH THEIR "A". THEY WERE NOT SURPRISED WITH THEIR GRADE.

VOCAB ZONE

COUNTER-CLAIM - NO, WINNING THE LOTTERY IS NOT A GOOD IDEA

REAL LIFE STORIES

SAY WHAT?

FILL IN THE BLANKS USING THE ADJECTIVES BELOW

DEPRESSED   HAPPY
EXTRAVAGANT   SECRETIVE
GUILTY   MISERABLE

THE NEW GIRL IS STRANGE. SHE DIDN'T TAKE OFF HER SUNGLASSES IN CLASS. THE TEACHER DIDN'T SAY ANYTHING ABOUT IT.

SHE WAS WRITING IN A SMALL NOTEBOOK. SHE'S A VERY _____ PERSON.

SOMEBODY STOLE MY PHONE TODAY IN GYM CLASS. THE POLICE FOUND THE PHONE IN LISA'S BAG!!!

LISA WAS _____ OF STEALING YOUR PHONE???

JENNIFER HAD AN _____ STRETCH WHITE LIMOUSINE FOR HER SWEET SIXTEEN PARTY.

JUSTIN BIEBER USED THE SAME LIMOUSINE.

WE PLAYED BASKETBALL AGAINST BRONX SCIENCE AND LOST. WE WERE _____

BRONX SCIENCE WON, 70-10. THEY WERE VERY _____.

NO ONE IS TALKING TO THE NEW KID. JASON BULLIED HIM AFTER SCHOOL.

THE NEXT DAY, HE LOOKED VERY _____ IN CLASS.

FACTS AND FIGURES

LOTTERIES HELP PAY FOR EDUCATION

A LOT OF PEOPLE BUY LOTTERY TICKETS. AFTER THE LOTTERY WINNER IS PAID, THERE IS SOME MONEY LEFT.

A RECENT POWERBALL LOTTERY WAS PLAYED IN 21 STATES. $380 MILLION IN TICKETS WERE SOLD. THE PRIZE WAS $280 MILLION.

THE GOVERNMENT CAN USE THIS MONEY FOR EDUCATION OR TO GIVE TO *SCHOOLS*.

STATE GOVERNMENTS WILL HAVE $100 MILLION FOR EDUCATION. STUDENTS WILL HAVE MORE MONEY FOR COMPUTERS, BOOKS, AND *FIELD TRIPS*.

WINNERS DO GOOD THINGS WITH THEIR EARNINGS

LOTTERY WINNERS USE THE MONEY TO HELP THEIR COMMUNITIES.

LES ROBBINS WAS A JUNIOR HIGH SCHOOL TEACHER. HE WON $111 MILLION IN 1993. HE CREATED A DAY CAMP FOR KIDS IN MALONE, WISCONSIN. HE CALLED IT "CAMP WINNEGATOR". KIDS CAN *RIDE HORSES*, GO SWIMMING, GO ON HIKES, AND PLAY MANY OUTDOOR SPORTS THERE.

THEY SPEND THE MONEY TO *BUILD* CAMPS, SUPERMARKETS, CHURCHES AND TO RENOVATE HOUSES.

IN 2012, MARY LOHSE WON A $202 MILLION POWERBALL JACKPOT. HER TOWN, BONDURANT, IOWA, DID NOT HAVE A SUPERMARKET. SHE USED THE MONEY TO BUILD A SUPERMARKET IN THE TOWN.

PLAYING THE LOTTERY IS EXCITING

MANY PEOPLE ENJOY PLAYING THE LOTTERY. PEOPLE PLAY THE LOTTERY WHEN THEY DON'T HAVE MONEY FOR MOVIES, GOING OUT TO DINNER, OR SPORTING EVENTS.

I WON $20!!!

ANYONE'S CHANCE OF WINNING A LOTTERY IS VERY SMALL (LESS THAN 1 IN 175 MILLION); HOWEVER, PEOPLE ARE EXCITED BY THE *DREAM* OF WINNING. MANY PEOPLE DON'T MIND BUYING $2 TICKETS.

THERE ARE LOTTERIES THAT RUN IN SEVERAL STATES AT ONCE WITH VERY LARGE PRIZES. THERE ARE LOTTERIES THAT PAY OUT MANY SMALL PRIZES. SMALL PRIZES KEEP PEOPLE PLAYING THE LOTTERY. PEOPLE ARE HAPPY EVEN IF THEY WIN A SMALL *PRIZE*.

FILL IN THE BLANKS USING THE FOLLOWING WORDS

RIDE HORSES	DREAM
SCHOOLS	FIELD TRIPS
BUILD	PRIZE

I NOW HAVE $114 MILLION. MY STATE GOVERNMENT CAN NOW GIVE THIS MONEY TO _____.

OUR STATE GOVERNMENT HAS LOTTERY MONEY. WE WILL USE THIS MONEY FOR COMPUTERS, BOOKS, AND _____.

AT THE CAMP, I CAN _____.

WE ARE _____ A SUPERMARKET.

ONE DAY MY _____ WILL COME TRUE.

HURRAY! I WON A _____.

VOCAB ZONE

FACTS AND FIGURES

GOVERNMENTS SAY THEY USE MONEY FOR EDUCATION, BUT THEY DON'T.

WHEN THE FIRST LOTTERIES WERE APPROVED, STATES PROMISED THAT THE MONEY WOULD GO TO SCHOOLS.

HOWEVER, MANY STATES NOW USE LOTTERY MONEY TO PAY FOR OTHER THINGS, TAKING MONEY AWAY FROM SCHOOLS. GOVERNMENTS USE LOTTERY MONEY TO "PATCH HOLES" IN THEIR *BUDGETS*.

SOME STATES USE LOTTERY MONEY FOR PUBLIC PARKS, PUBLIC TRANSPORTATION, AND *CONSERVATION* PROJECTS.

LOW-INCOME FAMILIES WASTE A LOT OF MONEY ON THE LOTTERY

POORER PEOPLE ARE SOMETIMES FOOLED BY WHAT'S CALLED THE "PEANUTS EFFECT." THEY TAKE MORE RISKS MORE FREQUENTLY WHEN THE PRICE OF AN ITEM IS LOW. LOWER INCOME PEOPLE OFTEN BUY MANY LOW-PRICED TICKETS AT A TIME.

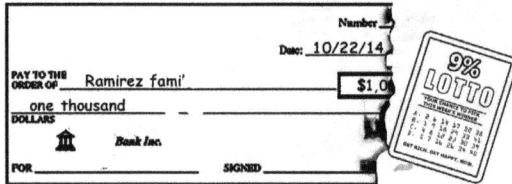

Number
Date: 10/22/14
PAY TO THE ORDER OF Ramirez fami' $1,0
one thousand
DOLLARS
Bank Inc.
FOR _____   SIGNED _____

9% LOTTO

A 2008 STUDY SHOWED THAT FAMILIES THAT MADE ABOUT $1,000 A MONTH SPENT MORE THAN 9% OF THEIR *INCOME* ON LOTTERY TICKETS.

LOTTERY MAKERS KNOW THIS, SO THEY CREATE MANY DIFFERENT KINDS OF *LOW-PRICED* GAMES. POOR PEOPLE THEN BUY MORE OF THESE CHEAPER GAME TICKETS. THEY OFTEN SPEND MORE MONEY ON GAMES THAN OTHER NEEDS.

ON THE CONTRARY, MANY WINNERS WIND UP BROKE OR WORSE

FORBES MAGAZINE REPORTS THAT 1% OF LOTTERY WINNERS GO BROKE. THIS IS DOUBLE THE NORMAL BANKRUPTCY RATE. SOME STUDIES SHOW THAT YEARS AFTER WINNING THE LOTTERY, MANY PEOPLE DO NOT FEEL MUCH HAPPIER THAN BEFORE.

DENISE ROSSI WON $1.3 MILLION. A YEAR LATER, SHE HAD TO DECLARE *BANKRUPTCY*.

BILLIE BOB HARELL, JR. WON $31 MILLION IN THE 1997 TEXAS LOTTO. TWENTY MONTHS AFTER WINNING. HE WAS FOUND DEAD WITH A GUNSHOT *wound* TO HIS HEAD.

BUDGET

CONSERVATION

SPENDING

MONEY

NATURE

PROTECTION

SALARY

CHEAP

NO MONEY

DEATH

INCOME

LOW-PRICED

BANKRUPTCY

WOUND

PLAN YOUR ARGUMENTATIVE ESSAY

Is Winning the Lottery a Good Idea?

INTRODUCTION

Thesis (claim): _____
_____
_____

BODY PARAGRAPHS

CLAIM PARAGRAPHS

Reason 1 - Topic Sentence: _____
_____

Evidence:
- _____
- _____
- _____

Reason 2 - Topic Sentence: _____

Evidence:
- _____
- _____
- _____

Reason 1 - Topic Sentence: _____
_____

Evidence:
- _____
- _____
- _____

COUNTER-CLAIM

Topic Sentence: _____
_____

Evidence:
- _____
- _____
- _____

CONCLUSION

Re-state Thesis (claim): _____
_____
_____

REAL LIFE STORIES

THE MILITARY PAYS FOR COLLEGE.

JOE SMITH SERVED FOUR YEARS IN THE NAVY AS A SONAR TECHNICIAN ON A SUBMARINE. HE SERVED IN THE PERSIAN GULF DURING OPERATION IRAQI FREEDOM.

AFTER SERVING FOUR YEARS, JOE WENT TO COLLEGE WITH THE HELP OF THE GI BILL. JOE NOW WORKS AT NASA AS AN ACOUSTICS ENGINEER.

THE MILITARY CHALLENGES YOU.

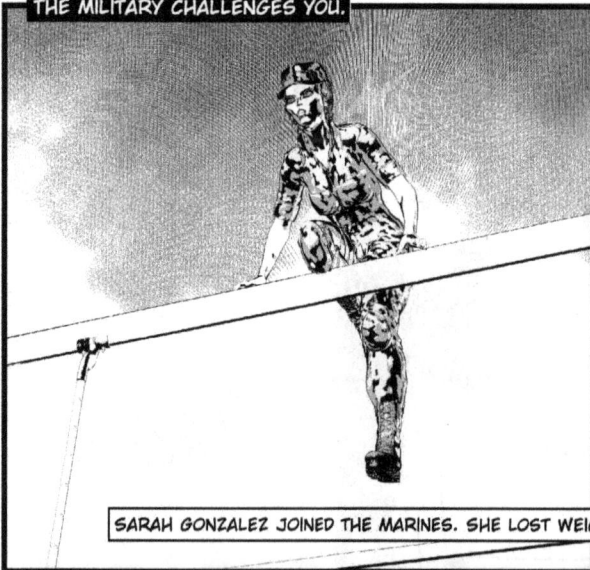

HEY- DROP TO THE GROUND AND GIVE ME 100 PUSH-UPS!!!!

SARAH GONZALEZ JOINED THE MARINES. SHE LOST WEIGHT, SHE BECAME FIT.

THE MILITARY GIVES YOU WORK EXPERIENCE AND HEALTH INSURANCE

GINA BRONSTEIN WAS A MILITARY SECURITY GUARD IN IRAQ. SHE GUARDED A MILITARY BASE.

HALT!!! MEDICAL INSURANCE CARD, PLEASE !!!

GINA IS NOW A PRIVATE SECURITY GUARD. SHE WORKS AT THE EMPIRE STATE BUILDING. SHE MAKES $47,000 A YEAR. SHE HAS MEDICAL INSURANCE.

HALT!!! I.D.'S OUT, PLEASE!!!

SONAR TECHNICIAN

ENGINEER

SOLDIER

SERGEANT

DOCTOR

SECURITY GUARD

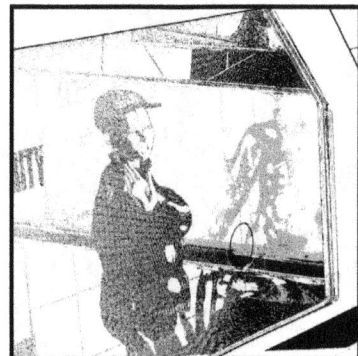

REAL LIFE STORIES

RECRUITERS LIE TO TEENS.

RECRUITERS PROMISE MILITARY CAREERS. HOWEVER, THE REALITY IS DIFFERENT.

LIFE, LIBERTY A — OF ALL WHO THREATEN IT.

MARK WAS TOLD THAT HE WOULD BE STATIONED IN GERMANY ON A BASE.

IN REALITY, HE WAS SENT TO FIGHT IN IRAQ AND WAS KILLED BY A ROADSIDE BOMB.

LEADERS LIE ABOUT REASONS FOR GOING TO WAR.

PAT TILLMAN WAS A SPORTS HERO WHO JOINED THE MILITARY AFTER THE 9/11 ATTACKS. HE WANTED TO HUNT BIN LADEN IN AFGHANISTAN.

HE WAS SENT TO IRAQ. HE FELT THAT THE IRAQ WAR WAS FOUGHT FOR OIL, NOT FOR THE FREEDOM OF THE IRAQI PEOPLE.

AFTER HE RETURNED FROM IRAQ, TILLMAN WAS SENT TO AFGHANISTAN WHERE HE WAS KILLED IN MYSTERIOUS CIRCUMSTANCES.

SOLDIERS COME BACK FROM WAR WITH PROBLEMS.

EDDIE RAY ROUTH CAME BACK FROM IRAQ WITH PTSD.

PTSD IS A SICKNESS THAT CAUSES NIGHTMARES, PHYSICAL PAIN, AND STRESS. HE FELT PHYSICAL PAIN EVEN WHEN HE WASN'T IN DANGER.

....HE KILLED CHRIS KYLE, A WAR HERO, WHEN THEY WERE BOTH PRACTICING SHOOTING.

MARK WAS PROMISED HE WOULD BE STATIONED IN GERMANY, BUT _____

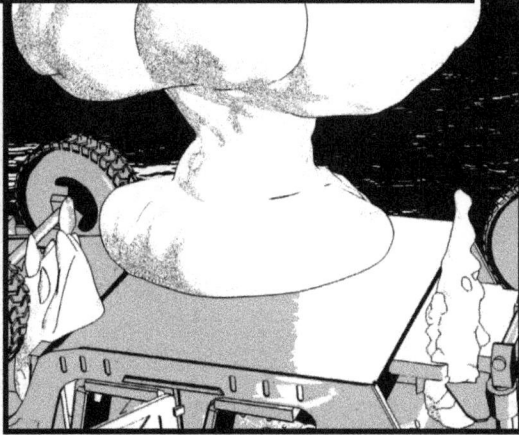

PAT TILLMAN WANTED TO FIGHT FOR THE FREEDOM OF THE IRAQI PEOPLE, BUT _____

CHRIS KYLE WAS A WAR HERO, BUT EDDIE RAY ROUTH _____

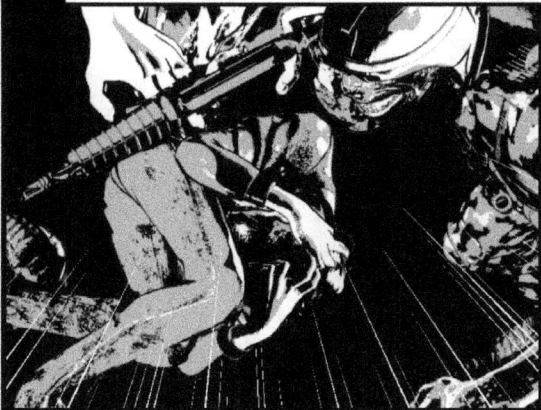

VOCAB ZONE

FACTS AND FIGURES

THE MILITARY IS A GREAT LEARNING EXPERIENCE - IT OFFERS TRAINING AND PAYS FOR COLLEGE.

IN 2009, THE GOVERNMENT CREATED A NEW "G.I. BILL". THIS BILL ALLOWS VETERANS TO RETURN TO SCHOOL FOR UP TO FOUR YEARS.

G.I. BILL

THE GOVERNMENT WILL PAY FOR TUITION, HOUSING, AND OTHER SCHOOL-RELATED COSTS.

EVERY YEAR, MORE THAN 700,000 FORMER SOLDIERS TAKE ADVANTAGE OF THIS OFFER.

BENEFIT

THE GOVERNMENT PAYS MORE THAN $12 BILLION A YEAR FOR THIS BENEFIT.

THE MILITARY TAKES PEOPLE AROUND THE WORLD.

THE U.S. MILITARY HAVE BASES AROUND THE WORLD. SOLDIERS ENJOY TRAVEL BENEFITS. SOLDIERS RECEIVE 30 DAYS OF PAID VACATION A YEAR.

VACATION

AIRCRAFT

MILITARY MEMBERS AND THEIR FAMILIES CAN TRAVEL ON MILITARY AIRCRAFT FOR FREE, AS WELL AS STAYING AT MILITARY BASES FOR FREE.

U.S. SOLDIERS ARE FIGHTING FOR FREEDOM AND DEMOCRACY.

FREEDOM

THE AMERICAN SOLDIER IS SOMETIMES KNOWN AS "THE WORLD'S POLICEMAN."

DEMOCRACY

IN A SEPT 17, 2013, NATIONAL REVIEW ARTICLE, THE JOURNALIST DENNIS PRAGER ARGUED THAT THERE IS NO OTHER COUNTRY THAN AMERICA THAT CAN PROMOTE DEMOCRACY AROUND THE WORLD.

WHY DOES THE GOVERNMENT PAY YOUR TUITION?

WHY WAS THE G.I.BILL CREATED?

WHY DO YOU NEED A VACATION?

WHY DO SOLDIERS AND THEIR FAMILIES TRAVEL FOR FREE?

WHY IS THE AMERICAN SOLDIER SOMETIMES CALLED "THE WORLD'S POLICEMAN"?

WHY DOES AMERICA PROMOTE DEMOCRACY AROUND THE WORLD?

VOCAB ZONE

20

COUNTER-CLAIM - NO, JOINING THE MILITARY IS NOT A GOOD IDEA.

FACTS AND FIGURES

WARS KILL PEOPLE.

THE GOAL OF THE SOLDIERS IN A WAR IS TO DEFEAT THE ENEMY. THIS MEANS THAT SOLDIERS KILL OTHER SOLDIERS AND SOMETIMES INNOCENT PEOPLE.

INNOCENT

FOR EVERY PERSON KILLED BY WAR, ANOTHER 10 ARE WOUNDED.

INNOCENT

ARMIES DO NOT TRAIN PEOPLE HOW TO THINK INDEPENDENTLY

DRILL

THE MILITARY TRAINS YOU TO TAKE ORDERS. SOLDIERS ARE DRILLED TO PERFORM TASKS WITHOUT THINKING, ACT AS A TEAM AND REACT QUICKLY IN EMERGENCY SITUATIONS.

REFLECTION

LIFE IS MORE COMPLEX. IT OFTEN REQUIRESS THINKING, OR REFLECTION, NOT IMMEDIATE ACTION.

MOST SOLDIERS DO NOT DO THE JOBS THEY ARE PROMISED BY RECRUITERS.

PEACEKEEPING

RECRUITERS TELL YOUNG PEOPLE THAT THEY WILL BE PARTICIPATING IN GLOBAL PEACEKEEPING OPERATIONS AND WILL USE TECHNOLOGICALLY ADVANCED WEAPONS.

MORE REALISTICALLY, MOST PEOPLE IN THE MILITARY SPEND MOST OF THEIR TIME DOING MAINTENANCE WORK: CLEANING, REPAIRING, AND TAKING APART VEHICLES, WEAPONS, AND SUPPLIES.

MAINTENANCE

FINISH THE SENTENCES USING THE FOLLOWING WORDS: REFLECTION, MAINTENANCE, INNOCENT PEOPLE.

21

IN A WAR, SOLDIERS KILL OTHER SOLDIERS, BUT SOMETIMES THEY KILL _____

IN THE ARMY, THEY TEACH YOU TO TAKE ORDERS, BUT IN REAL LIFE YOU HAVE TO USE _____

RECRUITERS TELL YOUNG PEOPLE THAT THEY WILL PARTICIPATE IN PEACEKEEPING OPERATIONS, BUT THEY DO _____

VOCAB ZONE

PLAN YOUR ARGUMENTATIVE ESSAY

Is Joining the Military a Good Idea?

INTRODUCTION

Thesis (claim): _____

_____

_____

BODY PARAGRAPHS

CLAIM PARAGRAPHS

Reason 1 - Topic Sentence: _____

_____

Evidence:
- _____
- _____
- _____

Reason 2 - Topic Sentence: _____

_____

Evidence:
- _____
- _____
- _____

Reason 1 - Topic Sentence: _____

_____

Evidence:
- _____
- _____
- _____

COUNTER-CLAIM

Topic Sentence: _____

_____

Evidence:
- _____
- _____
- _____

CONCLUSION

Re-state Thesis (claim): _____

_____

_____

HUMAN INTEREST STORIES

FACEBOOK IS POPULAR WORLDWIDE.

WORLDWIDE

WORLDWIDE, 1.35 BILLION PEOPLE USE FACEBOOK EVERY MONTH.

BECAUSE OF FACEBOOK'S POPULARITY, PARENTS HAVE NAMED THEIR CHILDREN "FACEBOOK" AND "LIKE."

LIKE

FACEBOOK

POPULAR

MARK ZUCKERBERG DONATES MONEY TO CHARITY.

THE INVENTOR OF FACEBOOK IS WORTH $17 BILLION. HE INTENDS TO GIVE AWAY, OR DONATE MOST OF HIS MONEY TO CHARITY.

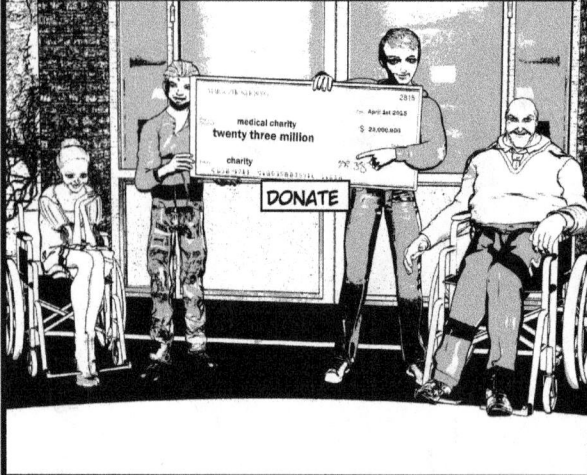

medical charity
twenty three million

charity

DONATE

ZUCKERBERG DONATED $100 MILLION TO NEWARK, NEW JERSEY SCHOOLS.

CHARITY

New Jersey Schools
one hundred million

charity

MIDDLETO
SCHO
GO
BUI
DO

MARK ZUCKERBERG IS A GENIUS.

GENIUS

HE STARTED WRITING COMPUTER PROGRAMS BEFORE HE TURNED 12. WHEN HE WAS IN HIGH SCHOOL, HE WAS ALREADY BEING RECRUITED BY SOFTWARE COMPANIES.

RISK

THE BIGGEST RISK IS NOT TAKING ANY RISK... IN A WORLD THAT IS CHANGING REALLY QUICKLY, THE ONLY STRATEGY THAT IS GUARANTEED TO FAIL IS NOT TAKING RISKS

WHY DO YOU SEE FRIENDS FROM OTHER COUNTRIES IN FACEBOOK? (WORLDWIDE)

WHY DO PARENTS NAME THEIR CHILDREN FACEBOOK AND LIKE? (POPULAR)

LIKE

WHY DO PEOPLE RESPECT MARK ZUCKERBERG? (DONATE)

medical charity
twenty three million $ 23.000.000

charity

HOW DOES HE HELP PEOPLE? (CHARITY)

New Jersey Schools
one hundred million

charity

WHY IS MARK ZUCKERBERG CALLED A GENIUS? (WRITES PROGRAMS)

WHY IS MARK ZUCKERBERG SUCCESSFUL? (TAKES RISKS)

VOCAB ZONE

HUMAN INTEREST STORIES

STEFANI JOANNE ANGELINA GERMANOTTA, A.K.A. LADY GAGA, IS A TALENTED SINGER, MUSICIAN, WRITER, AND BUSINESSWOMAN.

Paparazzi

Born This Way

MUSICIAN

Just Dance

LoveGame

Poker Face

Edge Of Glory

Alejandro

Telephone

LADY GAGA WRITES HER OWN SONGS.

SHE APPEARED AT THE 2010 MTV MUSIC AWARDS IN A DRESS MADE OUT OF MEAT.

MEAT

LADY GAGA IS A VERY SUCCESSFUL ARTIST.

AWARDS

LADY GAGA HAS SOLD MILLIONS OF RECORDS AND WON MANY AWARDS.

TIME

POWERFUL

SHE'S BEEN LISTED BY TIME AND FORBES MAGAZINE AS ONE OF THE WORLD'S MOST POWERFUL WOMEN.

LADY GAGA IS A ROLE MODEL FOR TEENS.

LADY GAGA DEVELOPED THE BORN THIS WAY FOUNDATION TO HELP KIDS FACE BULLYING.

BULLYING

LADY GAGA IS A STRONG SUPPORTER OF GAY RIGHTS.

SUPPORTIVE

FILL IN THE BLANKS WITH THE FOLLOWING ADJECTIVES:
DARING, POWERFUL, CARING, TALENTED, RESOLUTE, SUPPORTIVE

STEFANI GERMANOTTA WRITES HER OWN SONGS. SHE IS VERY _____.

LADY GAGA USED PIECES OF MEAT TO MAKE HER COSTUME. SHE IS _____.

LADY GAGA WORKS VERY HARD AND RECEIVED A LOT OF AWARDS. SHE IS _____.

TIME MAGAZINE RECOGNIZED LADY GAGA AS ONE OF THE MOST _____ WOMEN IN THE WORLD.

LADY GAGA FIGHTS TEEN BULLYING. HER FANS KNOW SHE IS A _____ PERSON.

_____ OF SEXUAL MINORITIES, LADY GAGA FIGHTS FOR THE RIGHTS OF GAY, BISEXUAL, AND TRANSGENDERED TEENS.

VOCAB ZONE

BIOGRAPHICAL ESSAY

MALALA YOUSAFZAI WAS BORN ON JULY 12, 1997, IN THE SWAT VALLEY, PAKISTAN. THERE, THE TALIBAN, A MUSLIM FUNDAMENTALIST GROUP, IS OPPOSED TO WOMEN RECEIVING EDUCATION.

THREATEN

THEY THREATEN GIRLS AND THEIR FAMILIES FOR ALLOWING THEM TO GO TO SCHOOL.

WHEN MALALA WAS A TEEN, SHE BLOGGED ABOUT THE CHALLENGES FACING GIRLS WHO WANTED TO GO TO SCHOOL IN THE AREA THREATENED BY THE TALIBAN.

BLOG

MALALA BECAME WELL-KNOWN IN PAKISTAN FOR HER BLOG.

IN OCTOBER 2012, TALIBAN MEMBERS BOARDED HER SCHOOL BUS AND SHOT AT HER AND TWO CLASSMATES.

SHOOT

SHOT IN THE HEAD, MALALA WAS FLOWN TO LONDON WHERE SHE MADE A RECOVERY. SHE BECAME A GLOBAL CAMPAIGNER FOR THE RIGHTS OF GIRLS TO RECEIVE AN EDUCATION.

CAMPAIGNER

AUTOBIOGRAPHY

I AM MALALA

MALALA RECEIVED MANY AWARDS FOR HER COURAGE. MALALA'S AUTOBIOGRAPHY I AM MALALA BECAME A WORLDWIDE BEST-SELLER.

IN 2013, MALALA BECAME THE YOUNGEST PERSON TO WIN THE NOBEL PEACE PRIZE.

NOBEL PEACE PRIZE

VOCAB ZONE

THREATENED/TALIBAN/BY/WAS/MALALA

BLOGGED/PAKISTAN/GIRLS/MALALA/ABOUT/IN/THE

SHOT/TALIBAN/MALALA/AT

AT/SPEECH/UN/THE/A/MADE/MALALA

PUBLISHED/MALALA/BOOK/A

WON/PRIZE/NOBEL/THE/MALALA/PEACE

BIOGRAPHY

LEBRON JAMES WAS BORN ON DEC. 30, 1984, IN AKRON, OHIO. WHEN HE WAS A FRESHMAN, HE LED HIS TEAM TO A 27-0 RECORD IN A DIVISION III STATE CHAMPIONSHIP.

TEAM

THE NEXT YEAR, HE AGAIN LED HIS TEAM TO WIN THE CHAMPIONSHIP. AFTER THAT, LEBRON JAMES STARTED GETTING NATIONAL ATTENTION.

AT 17, JAMES WAS ALREADY 6'8" AND WEIGHED 240 LBS. SEVERAL OF HIS HIGH SCHOOL GAMES WERE TELEVISED NATIONALLY AND HE APPEARED ON THE COVER OF SPORTS ILLUSTRATED.

CAVS 23

ATHLETE

BY HIS SENIOR YEAR, HE WAS CONSIDERED THE MOST SUCCESSFUL ATHLETE IN HIGH SCHOOL BASKETBALL HISTORY AND HE WAS DRAFTED BY THE CLEVELAND CAVALIERS.

IN THE NBA, LEBRON WAS THE YOUNGEST PLAYER TO EVER SCORE 40 POINTS IN A GAME. HE WAS ALSO THE YOUNGEST PERSON TO WIN ROOKIE OF THE YEAR.

CAVS

ROOKIE

THE DAILY STAR

ALL ABOUT THE BIG WORLD WE LIVE IN   EXCLUSIVE NEWS TODAY

JAMES HONORS TRAYVON

Heat don hoodies after teen's death

In libris graecis appetere mea. At vim odio lorem omnes, pri id iuvaret partiendo. Vivendo menandri et sed. Lorem volumus blandit cu has. Sit cu alia porro fuisset.
Ea pro natum invidunt repudiandae, his et facilisi vituperatoribus. Mei eu ubique altera senserit.
Ea pro natum invidunt repudiandae, his et facilisi vituperatoribus. Mei eu ubique altera senserit, consul eripuit accusata has ne. Ea pro natum invidunt repudiandae, his et facilisis vituperatoribus. Sed ut nunc adipiscing leo porttitor pharetra. Nam dictum. Mauris eu eros. Aenean vulputate dolor quis felis. Etiam

SOCIAL ISSUES

Wade posted a photo of himself from a previous photo shoot wearing a hooded sweatshirt, otherwise known as a hoodie, to his Twitter and

LEBRON JAMES HAS STOOD UP FOR SOCIAL ISSUES. HE PROTESTS AGAINST ISSUES LIKE THE KILLING OF TRAYVON MARTIN, THE RACIST COMMENTS OF NBA TEAM OWNER DONALD STERLING, THE SHOOTING OF TEEN MICHAEL BROWN, AND THE CHOKING DEATH OF ERIC GARNER.

ELECTION

LEBRON IS A STRONG SUPPORTER OF PRESIDENT OBAMA, DONATING TO HIS CAMPAIGN AND APPEARING WITH HIM DURING ELECTION SEASON.

JOURNALIST

THE DAILY BEAST

LEBRON/ALI
COMPARING THE TWO MEGASTARS

"DAILY BEAST" JOURNALIST ROBERT SILVERMAN COMPARED LEBRON TO MUHAMMAD ALI. MUHAMMAD ALI IS CONSIDERED ONE OF THE GREATEST ATHLETES AND ACTIVISTS OF MODERN TIMES.

WHY WAS LEBRON JAMES THE BEST PLAYER ON HIS TEAM?

WHAT ADVANTAGES DID LEBRON HAVE AS A TEEN ATHLETE?

IF YOU WERE A ROOKIE, WOULD YOU BE ABLE TO SCORE 40 POINTS IN A GAME?

DO YOU SUPPORT THE SAME SOCIAL ISSUES AS LEBRON? WHY AND WHY NOT?

WHICH CANDIDATE IN THE PRESIDENTIAL ELECTIONS WOULD YOU SUPPORT?

WHY DID JOURNALIST ROBERT SILVERMAN COMPARE LEBRON TO MUHAMMAD ALI?

THE DAILY BEAST

VOCAB ZONE

PLAN YOUR ARGUMENTATIVE ESSAY

Who is the Most Important Millennial?

Thesis (claim): _____
_____
_____

Reason 1 - Topic Sentence: _____
_____

Evidence: ▪ _____
_____
▪ _____
_____
▪ _____
_____

Reason 2 - Topic Sentence: _____
_____

Evidence: ▪ _____
_____
▪ _____
_____
▪ _____
_____

Reason 1 - Topic Sentence: _____
_____

Evidence: ▪ _____
_____
▪ _____
_____
▪ _____
_____

Topic Sentence: _____
_____

Evidence: ▪ _____
_____
▪ _____
_____
▪ _____
_____

Re-state Thesis (claim): _____
_____
_____

INTRODUCTION

BODY PARAGRAPHS

CLAIM PARAGRAPHS

COUNTER-CLAIM

CONCLUSION

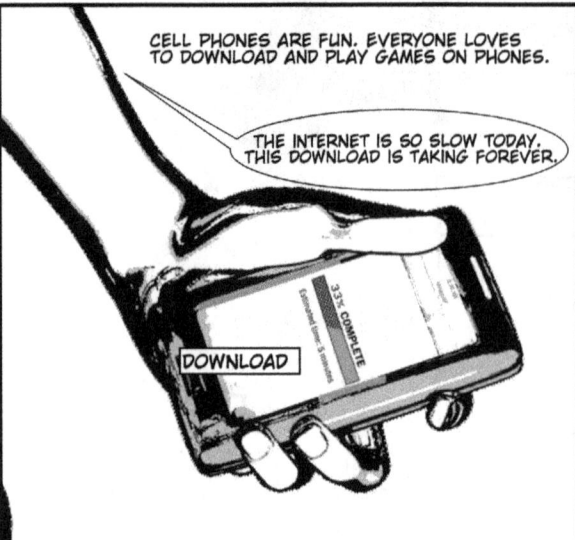

INFORMATIONAL EXCERPT

CONNECTION

SATELLITE

STREAM

CELLPHONE

WIKIPEDIA

DOWNLOAD

SHORT FOR CELLULAR PHONE- A PORTABLE TELEPHONE THAT USES WIRELESS TECHNOLOGY

THE ACTION OF LINKING ONE THING WITH ANOTHER

AN ONLINE ENCYCLOPEDIA/INFORMATION SOURCE

A CELESTIAL BODY ORBITING A PLANET OR STAR

TO COPY DATA FROM ONE COMPUTER TO ANOTHER, OR FROM THE INTERNET TO A COMPUTER

TO TRANSMIT OR RECEIVE DATA IN A STEADY, CONTINUOUS FLOW

VOCAB ZONE

AIRPLANES LET US TRAVEL AROUND THE WORLD QUICKLY AND CHEAPLY.

THE SEA VOYAGE BETWEEN EUROPE AND AMERICA USED TO TAKE BETWEEN 1 AND 2 WEEKS AND COST MORE THAN ONE MONTH'S SALARY.

STEAMER

TODAY, PEOPLE FLY BETWEEN NYC AND PARIS IN SEVEN HOURS. THE PRICE OF FLYING HAS BEEN CUT IN HALF IN THE LAST 30 YEARS. YOU CAN FLY ROUND TRIP FOR $600. FIFTY PERCENT OF AMERICANS TOOK TWO FLIGHTS LAST YEAR.

AIRPLANE

AIRPLANES TRANSPORT GOODS.

WOW! THOSE ARE EXPENSIVE SNEAKERS!

TRANSPORT AND SHIP

NIKE DESIGNS SNEAKERS IN PORTLAND, OREGON, AND ASSEMBLES THEM IN CHINA, VIETNAM, AND INDONESIA. THE SNEAKERS ARE SHIPPED BY AIR FREIGHT AROUND THE WORLD.

APPLE DESIGNS THE IPHONE IN CUPERTINO, CALIFORNIA. PARTS OF AN IPHONE COME FROM NINE DIFFERENT COMPANIES IN CHINA, TAIWAN, SOUTH KOREA, JAPAN, AND THE U.S. THE PHONE IS ASSEMBLED IN CHINA, AND DELIVERED TO COUNTRIES ALL OVER THE WORLD.

CALIFORNIA   TAIWAN   SOUTH KOREA   JAPAN   USA

ASSEMBLED

AIRPLANES ARE USED IN WARS AND EMERGENCIES.

AIRPLANES ARE USED TO FIGHT FOREST FIRES AND RESCUE PEOPLE.

RESCUE

PILOTLESS PLANES CALLED "DRONES" HUNT DOWN TERRORISTS IN THE MIDDLE EAST

BZZZZZZZ!

DRONES

INFORMATIONAL EXCERPT

ON THE STEAMER, IT WOULD TAKE YOU TWO WEEKS TO TRAVEL TO EUROPE; ON THE AIRPLANE, _____ _____.

VERY FEW PEOPLE COULD TAKE A SEA VOYAGE - IT WAS EXPENSIVE; BUT BY AN AIRPLANE _____ _____.

NIKE SNEAKERS ARE DESIGNED IN THE US, BUT _____ _____.

PEOPLE DIDN'T HAVE GOODS FROM OTHER COUNTRIES, BUT NOW AIRPLANES _____

A LOT OF PEOPLE USED TO DIE IN FLOOD AND FOREST FIRES, BUT NOW _____ _____.

A LOT OF MILITARY PILOTS WERE KILLED IN WARS BEFORE, BUT NOW _____

VOCAB ZONE

SCIENCE ARTICLE

PENICILLIN IS THE MOST WIDELY-USED ANTIBIOTIC IN THE WORLD.

PENICILLIN

PENICILLIN WAS DISCOVERED BY MISTAKE IN SEPTEMBER 1928 BY DR. ALEXANDER FLEMING, A BACTERIOLOGIST WORKING IN LONDON. IT REDUCES THE THREAT OF BACTERIAL INFECTIONS. MILLIONS OF PEOPLE NOW SURVIVE INFECTIONS THAT USED TO BE DEADLY.

PENICILLIN IS USED TO TREAT DISEASES THAT SPREAD THROUGH INFECTION

DISEASE

SUCH DISEASES AS SYPHILIS, MENINGITIS, AND PNEUMONIA CAN BE TREATED THANKS TO PENICILLIN'S ABILITY TO STOP THE GROWTH OF DANGEROUS BACTERIA. PENICILLIN IS ALSO USED IN THE TREATMENT OF BURNS.

THE DISCOVERY OF PENICILLIN HAS ALLOWED FOR ADVANCES IN SURGERY.

SURGERY

DOCTORS CAN PERFORM OPERATIONS, ORGAN TRANSPLANTS, AND OPEN HEART SURGERY THANKS TO PENICILLIN'S HELP IN FIGHTING INFECTIONS.

PENICILLIN HAS LED TO THE SYNTHESIS OF NEW ANTIBIOTICS.

INFECTION

DOZENS OF NEW ANTIBIOTICS SUCH AS STREPTOMYCIN (FOR TUBERCULOSIS), CEPHALOSPORIN (FOR MENINGITIS), AND GRISEOFULVIN (FOR SKIN INFECTIONS) WERE FOUND AS A RESULT OF PENICILLIN'S DISCOVERY.

PENICILLIN WAS USED WIDELY BY ALLIED DOCTORS IN WORLD WAR II.

INJURIES

ALTHOUGH DISCOVERED IN 1928, ITS USE BY ARMY DOCTORS ALLOWED SOLDIERS TO SURVIVE AND RECOVER FROM INJURIES THAT WOULD HAVE KILLED THEM.

PENICILLIN IS STILL USED TODAY.

BACTERIA

HOWEVER, BACTERIA ARE CONSTANTLY MUTATING. DOCTORS RACE AGAINST MUTATIONS TO CREATE EFFECTIVE NEW ANTIBIOTICS.

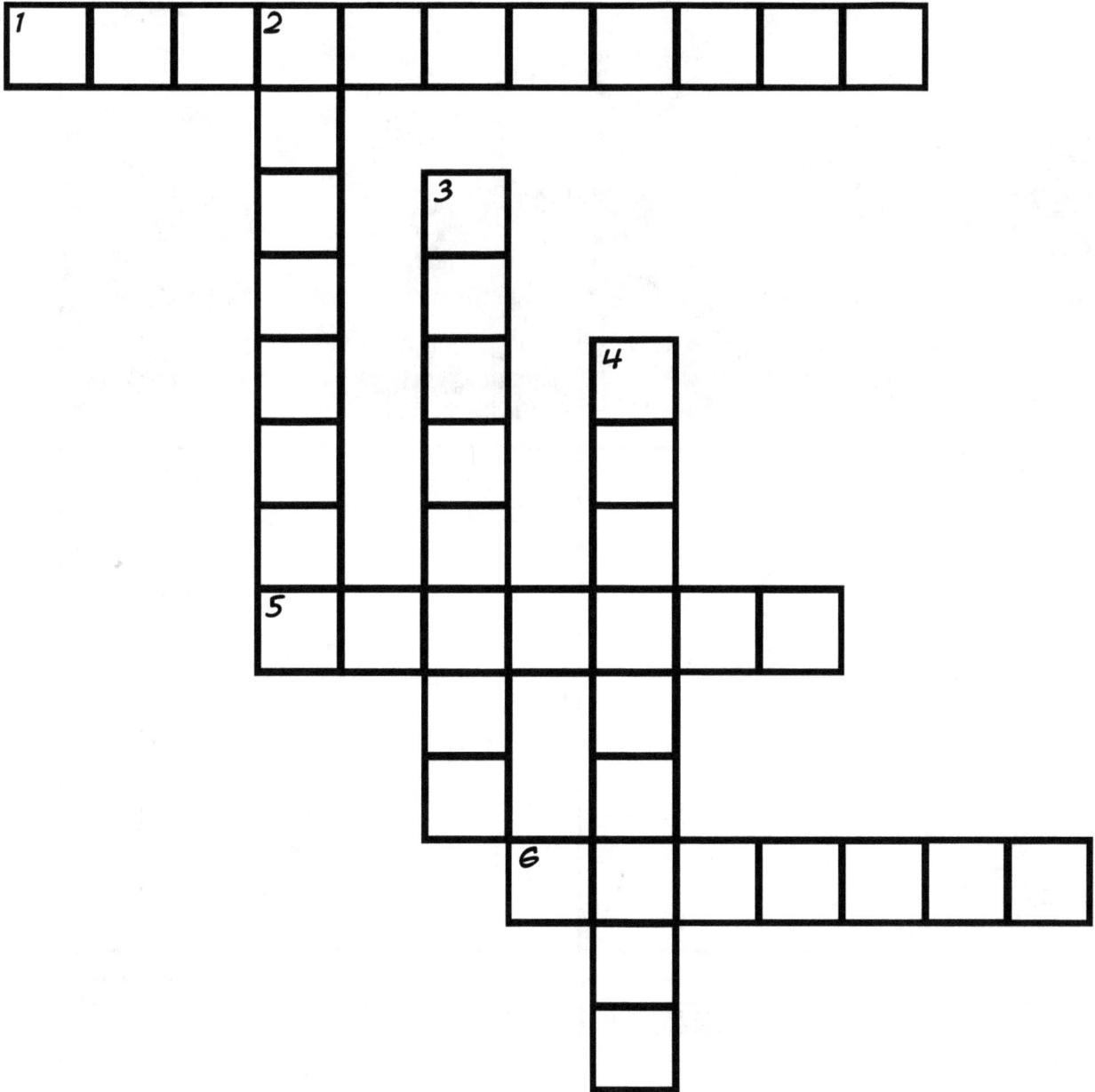

VOCAB ZONE

ACROSS

1. a medicine that destroys harmful bacteria
5. the practice of treating illness and diseases
6. illness or abnormal condition

DOWN

2. physical harm done to living things
3. very small organisms found everywhere
4. contamination with germs or disease

SCIENCE ARTICLE

ROBOT

IN 2000, HONDA OF JAPAN CREATED A HUMANOID ROBOT, "ASIMO". THE UN ESTIMATES THAT MORE THAN 750,000 INDUSTRIAL ROBOTS ARE BEING USED WORLDWIDE, HALF OF THEM IN JAPAN.

IN 2004, EPSOM RELEASES A "FLYING ROBOT", A DRONE PROTOTYPE, TO HELP FILM NATURAL DISASTERS.

NATURAL DISASTER

IN 2006, A ROBOTIC SURGEON PERFORMED A 50-MINUTE OPERATION ON A 34 YEAR-OLD MAN'S HEART.

SCALPEL, GAUZE, SCISSORS!

SURGEON

IN 2009, RESEARCHERS AT CAMBRIDGE UNIVERSITY IN LONDON CREATED ADAM, A ROBOT CAPABLE OF LEARNING. ADAM WAS ABLE TO READ, DESIGN LAB EXPERIMENTS, AND CARRY THEM OUT.

EXPERIMENT

IN 2012, SCIENTISTS CREATED A ROBOT ARM. THE PATIENT HAS A CHIP IN HER HEAD. THE ROBOT ARM IS OPERATED BY THE CHIP.

I WANT SOME WATER.

CHIP

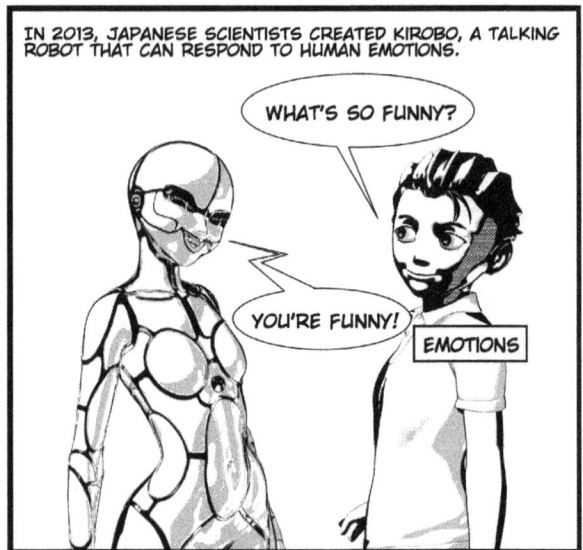

IN 2013, JAPANESE SCIENTISTS CREATED KIROBO, A TALKING ROBOT THAT CAN RESPOND TO HUMAN EMOTIONS.

WHAT'S SO FUNNY?

YOU'RE FUNNY!

EMOTIONS

FILL IN THE BLANKS WITH THE VOCABULARY WORDS: CHIP, EXPERIMENT, NATURAL DISASTERS, EMOTIONS, ROBOTIC SURGEON, ROBOT.

HUMANS HAVE ALWAYS IMAGINED BUILDING MACHINES THAT COULD ACT LIKE THEM. SOME PEOPLE BELIEVE THAT ONE DAY _____ MIGHT TAKE OVER THE PLANET!

EARTHQUAKES, TSUNAMIS, FLOODS, AND MUDSLIDES CAN ALL BE TRAGEDIES. THESE ARE ALL EXAMPLES OF _____.

IN THE FUTURE A _____ MIGHT PERFORM AN OPERATION ON A PATIENT WHO IS IN A HOSPITAL IN A SECOND COUNTRY.

SCIENTISTS USE AN _____ TO TEST HYPOTHESES. THESE _____s MUST BE REPEATABLE BY OTHER SCIENTISTS FOR A HYPOTHESES TO BE PROVEN AS TRUE.

INSIDE OF YOUR SMARTPHONE, IS A _____ THAT IS THE "BRAIN" OF ANY COMPUTING DEVICE.

ROBOTS CAN NOT ONLY RESPOND TO HUMAN _____, BUT ALSO CAN SHOW _____ THEMSELVES, LIKE SMILING OR BEING SAD.

VOCAB ZONE

PLAN YOUR ARGUMENTATIVE ESSAY

What is the Greatest Invention of Modern Times?

Thesis (claim): _____
_____
_____

Reason 1 - Topic Sentence: _____
_____

Evidence: ▪ _____
_____

▪ _____
_____

▪ _____
_____

Reason 2 - Topic Sentence: _____
_____

Evidence: ▪ _____
_____

▪ _____
_____

▪ _____
_____

Reason 1 - Topic Sentence: _____
_____

Evidence: ▪ _____
_____

▪ _____
_____

▪ _____
_____

Topic Sentence: _____
_____

Evidence: ▪ _____
_____

▪ _____
_____

▪ _____
_____

Re-state Thesis (claim): _____
_____
_____

CHAPTER 5: IS IT A GOOD IDEA FOR TEENS TO GET TATTOOS?

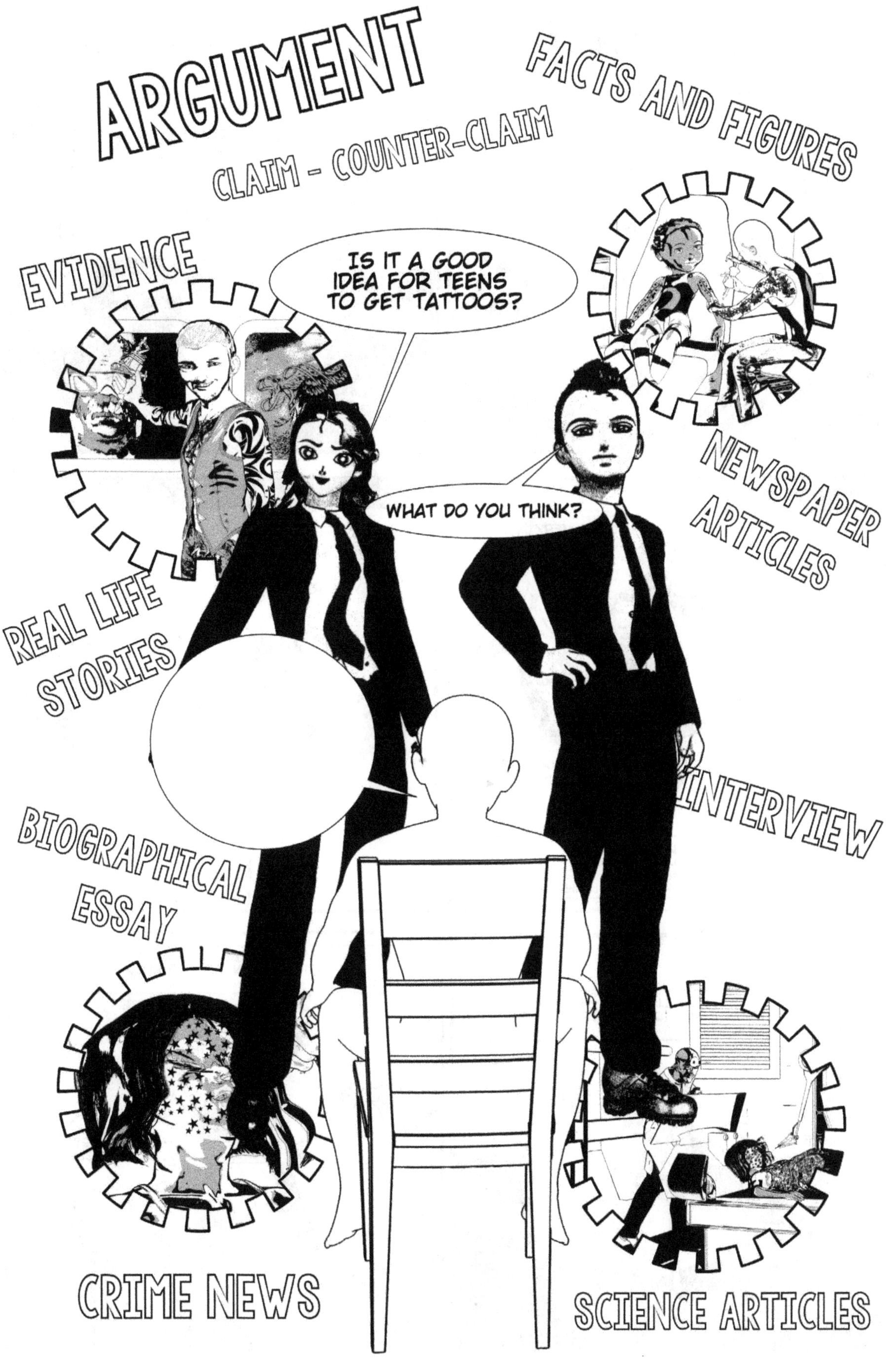

MAGAZINE ARTICLE

IT'S THE TIME IN LIFE TO EXPERIMENT.

CYNDY AND HER FRIEND JAMES MAKE THEIR OWN CLOTHES. THEY ALSO MAKE JEWELRY AND COLOR THEIR HAIR. THEY DESIGNED THEIR OWN TATTOOS AND HAD THEM DONE BY A PROFESSIONAL TATTOO ARTIST.

IT LOOKS GREAT!

ARRRRRGH!!!!!

TATTOO

THEIR PARENTS LOVE AND SUPPORT THEM. THEY TELL THEM THAT THIS IS THE TIME OF THEIR LIVES TO TRY NEW THINGS. CYNDY AND JAMES ARE APPLYING TO FASHION HIGH SCHOOLS IN NEW YORK CITY. THEY WANT TO BECOME DESIGNERS.

WE'RE SO PROUD OF YOU, GUYS!!!!

SCHOOL OF DESIGN

SUPPORT

TATTOOS ARE ART.

YOU'RE VERY FAMOUS!!!

YOU'RE THE BEST TATTOO ARTIST IN THE WORLD!!!

TATTOO ARTIST

SCOTT CAMPBELL IS ONE OF THE HIGHEST PAID TATTOO ARTISTS IN THE WORLD. HE CHARGES $1,000 FOR THE FIRST HOUR AND $200 FOR EACH SUCCEEDING ONE. MANY CELEBRITIES HAVE HIS TATTOOS.

HERE ARE SOME EXAMPLES OF SCOTT CAMPBELL'S DESIGNS....

THEY'RE RAD!!!

DESIGN

YOUR BODY IS YOUR OWN

DORIS LEE HAD SEVERAL ILLNESSES GROWING UP. SHE WAS ALWAYS GOING TO THE HOSPITAL AND GETTING INJECTIONS.

I HATE GETTING POKED BY NEEDLES!!!!

INJECTION

FOR SEVERAL YEARS, SHE BEGGED HER MOM FOR A DANDELION TATTOO. WHEN DORIS TURNED 17, HER MOM SAID "OK".

DANDELION

I LOVED GETTING POKED BY NEEDLES!!!

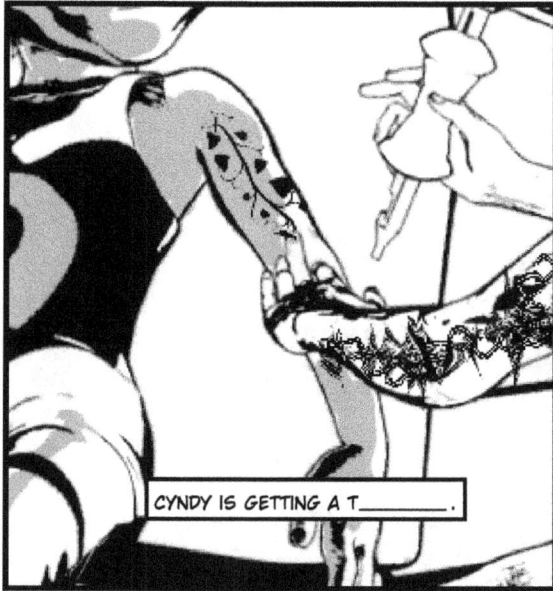

CYNDY IS GETTING A T_____.

CYNDY'S AND JAMES' PARENTS S_____THEM.

SCOTT CAMPBELL IS A T_____A_____.

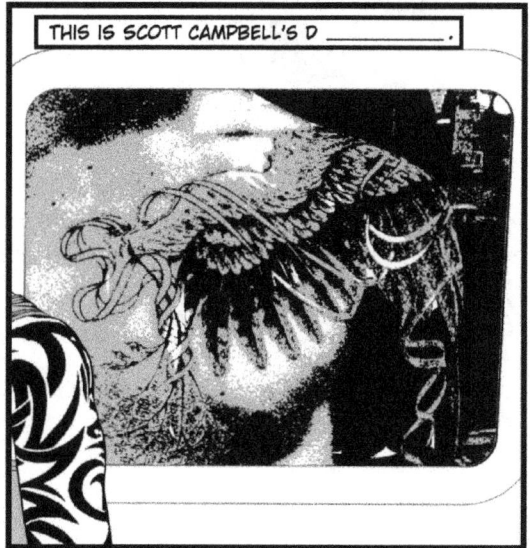

THIS IS SCOTT CAMPBELL'S D_____.

DORIS IS GETTING AN I _____.

NOW DORIS IS GETTING A D_____TATTOO.

VOCAB ZONE

CRIME NEWS

TATTOOS ARE PAINFUL AND EXPENSIVE TO REMOVE

18-YEAR-OLD KIMBERLEY VLAEMINCK OF KORTRIJK, BELGIUM, HAD 53 STARS TATTOOED ON HER FACE. SHE TOLD NEWSPAPERS THAT IT WAS A MISTAKE. SHE ASKED FOR THREE SMALL STARS. SHE FELL ASLEEP DURING THE SESSION. WHEN SHE WORK UP, SHE SAW 53 STARS ON HER FACE.

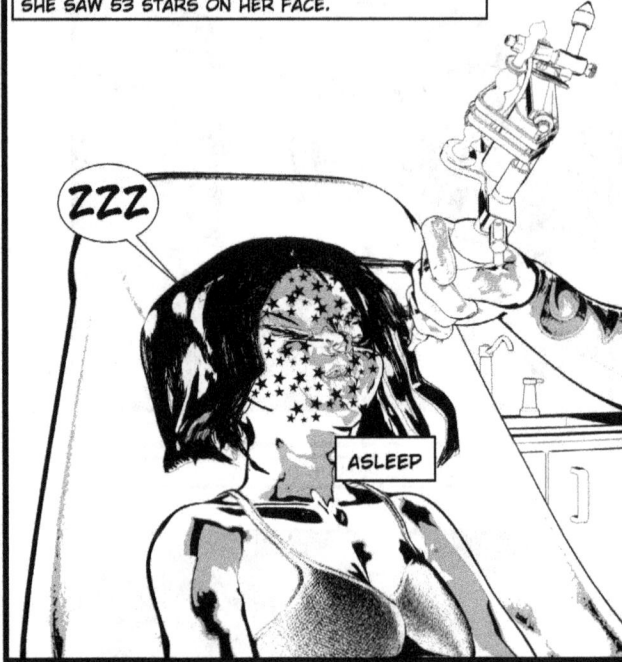

ZZZ

ASLEEP

SHE CLAIMED THAT THE TATTOO ARTIST DID NOT UNDERSTAND HER. THE RUSSIAN TATTOO ARTIST WAS FIRED AND MOVED BACK TO RUSSIA. KIMBERLEY LATER ADMITTED THAT SHE HAD LIED BECAUSE SHE WAS AFRAID OF HER FATHER'S OPINION. AFTER THREE YEARS, SHE STILL HAS FAINT STARS ON HER FACE.

YOU'RE FIRED!!!!

FIRED

JACKSON ROSWELL, 19, OF PORTSMOUTH, ENGLAND, WAS ARRESTED FOR TATTOOING THE NECK OF A 13-YEAR-OLD GIRL. UNFORTUNATELY, HE ALSO MADE A SPELLING MISTAKE WITH THE WORD "BELIEVE", SPELLING IT "B-E-L-L-E-V-E".

BELIEVE

ARE YOU SURE THAT'S HOW YOU SPELL "BELIEVE"?

THE FAMILY OF THE CHILD WAS FURIOUS. SHE WAS TAKEN TO A HOSPITAL AND JACKSON WAS ARRESTED. HE WAS GIVEN AN EIGHT-MONTH PRISON SENTENCE, A FINE, AND COMMUNITY SERVICE TO DO. THE CHILD HAD LASER SURGERY TO REMOVE THE TATTOO.

I HATED SPELLING IN SCHOOL!!!

ARRESTED

ANSWER THE QUESTIONS USING EVIDENCE FROM THE PANELS

HOW DID KIMBERLEY GET 53 TATTOO STARS ON HER FACE?

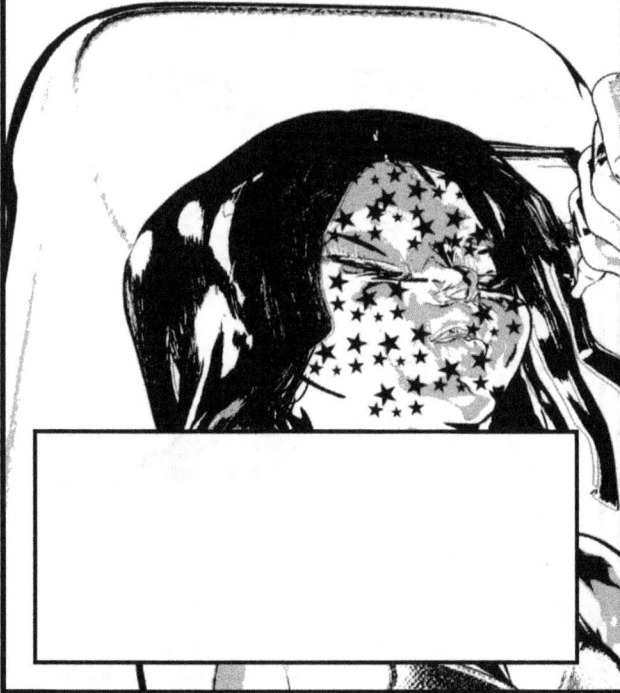

WHY DID SHE LIE TO THE NEWSPAPERS?

WHY WAS JACKSON ROSWELL ARRESTED?

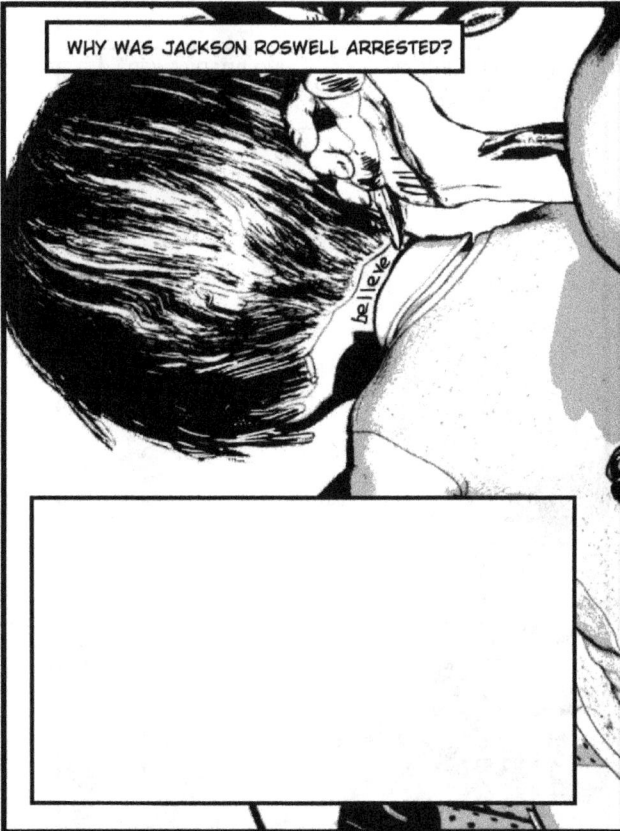

DO YOU THINK IT WAS FAIR TO SEND JACKSON TO PRISON?

VOCAB ZONE

FACTS AND FIGURES

MOST TEENS WILL REGRET IT LATER.

TATTOO REMOVAL CLINICS ARE MAKING MORE THAN $2.3 BILLION A YEAR. A RECENT SURVEY SHOWED THAT MORE THAN ⅛ OF PEOPLE WHO HAVE TATTOOS WANT TO GET THEM REMOVED.

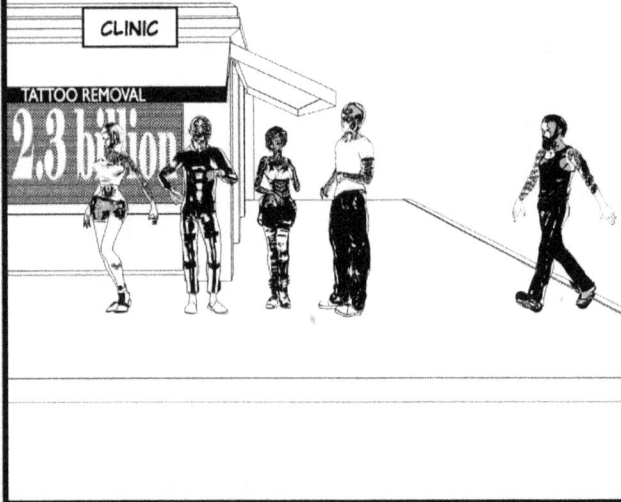

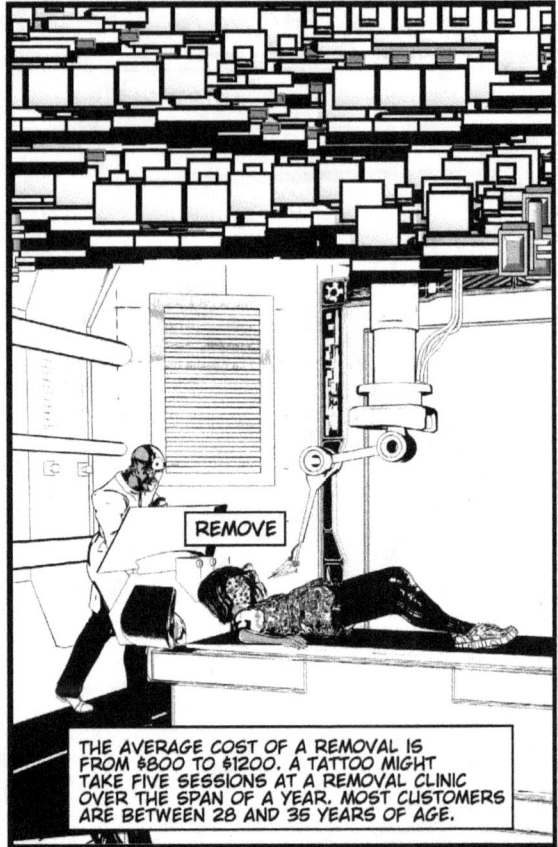

CLINIC

TATTOO REMOVAL

2.3 billion

REMOVE

THE AVERAGE COST OF A REMOVAL IS FROM $800 TO $1200. A TATTOO MIGHT TAKE FIVE SESSIONS AT A REMOVAL CLINIC OVER THE SPAN OF A YEAR. MOST CUSTOMERS ARE BETWEEN 28 AND 35 YEARS OF AGE.

IT MIGHT BE HARD TO FIND A JOB IF YOU HAVE A TATTOO.

IN 2013, LASER TATTOO REMOVAL BUSINESSES SAW A 32% INCREASE IN SALES. MOST OF THEIR BUSINESS CAME FROM REMOVING TATTOOS FROM PEOPLE'S FACES AND NECKS.

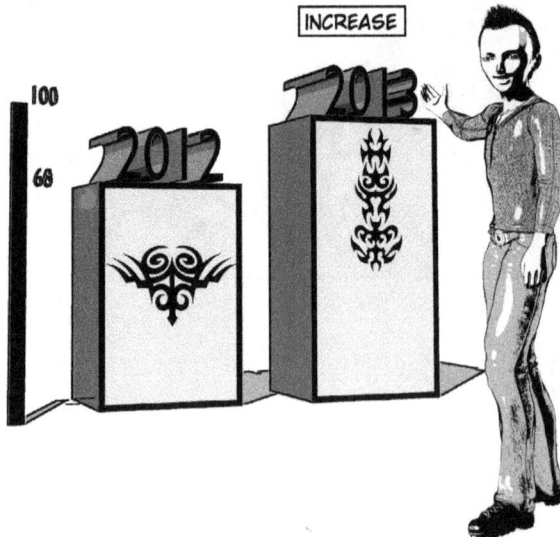

INCREASE

100

68

2012

2013

NINETY PERCENT OF BOSSES WHO INTERVIEWED PEOPLE AT JOB FAIRS SAID THEY WOULD PREFER TO HIRE A PERSON WITHOUT A VISIBLE TATTOO.

INTERVIEW

IN YOUR SCHOOL, 20 STUDENTS HAD TATTOOS. ONE FIFTH (⅕) OF THEM DECIDED TO HAVE THEM REMOVED. HOW MANY STUDENTS GOT THEIR TATTOOS REMOVED?

EACH REMOVAL SESSION IS $1,200. KIMBERLEY HAD 5 REMOVAL SESSIONS. HOW MUCH DID HER PARENTS PAY ALL TOGETHER?

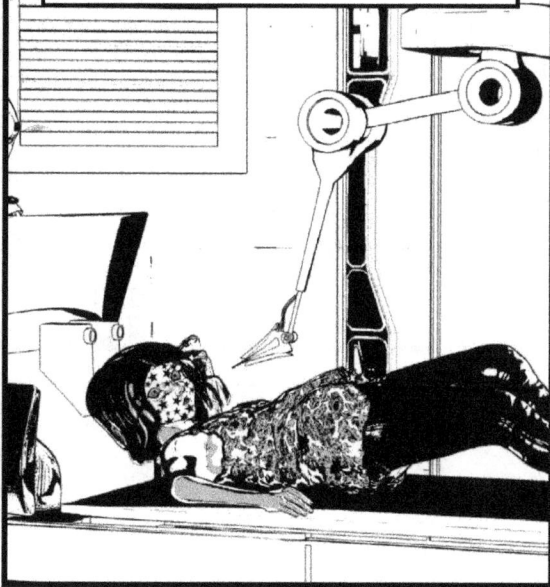

IN 2012, THE CLINIC REMOVED 1,000 TATTOOS. HOW MANY DID THEY REMOVE IN 2013?

WHAT PERCENT OF BOSSES HIRE PERSONS WITH VISIBLE TATTOOS?

VOCAB ZONE

50

INTERVIEW WITH ALEXA, A 17-YEAR-OLD STUDENT AT ELIZABETH IRWIN SCHOOL.

INTERVIEW

VOCAB ZONE

PLAN YOUR ARGUMENTATIVE ESSAY

Is it a Good Idea for Teens to Get Tattoos?

Thesis (claim): _____

_____

_____

Reason 1 - Topic Sentence: _____

_____

Evidence: ▪ _____

_____

▪ _____

_____

▪ _____

_____

Reason 2 - Topic Sentence: _____

_____

Evidence: ▪ _____

_____

▪ _____

_____

_____

▪ _____

_____

Reason 1 - Topic Sentence: _____

_____

Evidence: ▪ _____

_____

▪ _____

_____

▪ _____

_____

Topic Sentence: _____

_____

Evidence: ▪ _____

_____

▪ _____

_____

▪ _____

_____

Re-state Thesis (claim): _____

_____

_____

THE LOTTERY

1. If a student wanted to support a claim that "lottery money helps public school students achieve academically," he/she would find which piece of data most helpful:

A) A report comparing student ELA test scores nationwide

B) A graph showing how lottery money is used within New York State

C) An article about immigrant student gains on ESL tests

D) An article that ranks colleges around the world

2. An example of the "peanuts effect" influencing habits would be:

A) A student who drops out of school to work in a factory

B) A family buying a house they cannot afford, then moving to an apartment

C) A child spending his lunch money on peanut candy

D) A gambler spending $1,000 on a game, $1 at a time

3. Which is more likely to occur:

A) Being struck by lightning (US, 2014): 267 persons out of 318,000,000

B) Dying in a plane crash: 1 in 11,000,000

C) Attacked by an alligator: 2.6 in 1,000,000

D) A high school basketball player becoming a professional basketball player : 1 in 3,226

4. Which lottery winner best fits the description of someone "giving back to their community":

A) A man who buys a private jet, yacht, and limousine for his transportation

B) A woman who spends her winnings on plastic surgery and a weight reduction operation

C) A lottery winner who finances the construction of a statue of himself

D) A woman who builds a hospital with her earnings

5. Which is an unlikely reason for a person to buy a lottery ticket:

A) They feel themselves to be lucky

B) They enjoy the excitement of playing games

C) They have a strategy to pick the likely numbers

D) They think lottery tickets are a good investments

JOINING THE MILITARY

1. Which is an example of a military skill that became a civilian career:

    A) A navy sailor becomes a gourmet chef

    B) A marine soldier becomes a carpenter

    C) An air force pilot becomes a commercial airline captain

    D) An army cook becomes a mechanic

2. Which is an unlikely reason for joining the military:

    A) A boy cannot find job after high school

    B) A girl would like to pursue a career in nursing

    C) A student enjoys playing computer games involving combat

    D) Two friends would like to open a skateboarding shop together

3. Both Pat Tillman and Chris Kyle:

    A) Became heroes after they returned from war zones

    B) Died in unexpected circumstances

    C) Had second thoughts about their roles in war

    D) Had been heroes before they were soldiers

4. The G.I. Bill pays for:

    A) Students to enlist in the armed forces

    B) Women to make the same amount as men

    C) Former soldiers to afford the costs of college

    D) The cost of military weapons such as guns and tanks

5. Many times in life, persons are expected to "act quickly". In which situations, would this be appropriate:

    A) Deciding to marry someone you've just met

    B) Choosing the first college that accepts your application

    C) Accepting the advice from your friends on what clothes to wear

    D) Leaving a house on fire

MOST IMPORTANT MILLENNIAL

1. Which is an example of risk taken by Mark Zuckerberg, as reflected in his quote, "The biggest risk is not taking any risk... In a world that is changing really quickly, the only strategy that is guaranteed to fail is not taking risks.":

A) Dropping out of university

B) Being recruited by software companies

C) Donating money to charity

D) Writing software

2. In the following mission statement from Lady Gaga's Born This Way Foundation, what does the phrase, "shine a light" mean: "Born This Way Foundation is committed to supporting the wellness of young people, and empowering them to create a kinder and braver world. We achieve this by shining a light on real people, quality research and authentic partnerships."

A) Her fans will be seen in her music videos

B) Lights will be flashed at her concerts

C) Only quality people can participate in her foundation

D) Stories of students will be featured on her website

3. Which statement most closely reflects Malala Yousafzai's views on education:

A) Girls should receive a basic education. Their place is in the home.

B) Boys and girls should receive different instruction, in separate schools.

C) The views of religious fundamentalists should be respected in all questions of education.

D) Education should be for everyone, regardless of religion or gender.

4. "I'm not going to fight because I mean too much to our team, and I can't afford to be suspended for a game or do something stupid to get me kicked out of a playoff game." In this quote by LeBron James, James shows that he realizes:

A) His individual actions will directly affect outcomes for the people around him.

B) He is not responsible for the behaviors of others.

C) He must put his own needs ahead of those of his team mates.

D) He has a bright future off the basketball court.

5. Mark Zuckerberg, Lady Gaga, Malala Yousafzai, and LeBron James all share:

A) Political beliefs

B) Religious views

C) Personal style

D) Media recognition

NYS ELA-STYLE MULTIPLE CHOICE QUESTIONS

GREATEST INVENTION OF MODERN TIMES

1. **"The curved screen is a bold attempt to redefine the way smartphones are designed and used."** This quote, as part of an advertisement for the Samsung Galaxy S6, shows an example of

   A) exaggeration

   B) metaphor

   C) simile

   D) symbolism

2. **"Today we live in a world shaped by airplanes. Almost everything you buy, eat, wear, and use has been shipped by air. Airplanes allow people to live, work, and travel around the world. People go to places in hours instead of months. Airplanes can also be used to rescue people or to fight wars against enemies. For all these reasons, the airplane is the most important invention."** In this example introductory paragraph, what is the purpose of the second sentence?

   A) to state the thesis

   B) to expand on the meaning of the opening sentence

   C) to introduce the counterclaim

   D) this is the topic sentence

3. **From the feature on penicillin, it is reasonable to assume that:**

   A) researchers will continue to synthesize new antibiotics

   B) bacteria will refuse to mutate any further

   C) the world has conquered most medical problems

   D) students should not be immunized against diseases

4. **Which statement is supported by sufficient evidence by the feature on robots:**

   A) robots have taken over the world

   B) robot technology continues to advance

   C) soon all classrooms will have robot teachers

   D) robots cannot understand emotions

5. **The cellphone, airplane, robot, and penicillin all:**

   A) have created more problems than they have solved

   B) made life more difficult for most people

   C) slowed the pace of progress for generations of people

   D) increased communication, travel, mechanization, and health

TATTOOS FOR TEENS

1. From the feature about Cyndy and James getting tattoos, we can infer that:

A) Their close friends will not approve of their new tattoos

B) They will probably change their career ambitions and join the military

C) They will be forced to leave their homes

D) They will continue to explore their creativity

2. Scott Campbell could be described as:

A) Talented and ambitious

B) Derivative and lazy

C) Funny and friendly

D) Angry and cheap

Match these popular tattoo quotes with their meanings:

Quotes:

A) Fate fell short

B) i listened to the bray of my heart.. i am i am i am

C) Emancipate yourself from mental slavery

D) Be the one to guide me, but never hold me down

E) I am enough the way I am…

F) Beneath Lay Words That Suffocate

G) There Are No Rules That Can Bind You When You Find Your Other Half

H) I mourn for those who never know you

I) Do not go gentle into that good night, Rage, rage against the dying of the light

Meanings:

1) When you've found true love, nothing can keep you apart.

2) I will overcome the pains in my heart.

3) Help me, but don't hold me back.

4) Be careful with what you say- words can hurt.

5) Fight for your dreams.

6) Don't let others tell you how to live.

7) There must be another plan for you.

8) Be happy with who you are.

9) It's other people's loss to not know who you really are.

THE LOTTERY

Adams, Susan. "Why Winning Powerball Won't Make You Happy." Forbes. Forbes Magazine, 28 Nov. 2012. Web. 24 Oct. 2015.

Carbone, Nick. "$500 Million Powerball Jackpot: The Tragic Stories of the Lottery's Unluckiest Winners." *The Tragic Stories of the Lottery's Unluckiest Winners Comments.* N.p., 27 Nov. 2012. Web. 24 Oct. 2015.

Piore, Adam. "Why We Keep Playing the Lottery - Issue 17: Big Bangs - Nautilus." *Nautilus.* N.p., 25 Sept. 2014. Web. 24 Oct. 2015.

Popken, Ben. "Poor People Spend 9% Of Income On Lottery Tickets." *Consumerist.* N.p., 26 May 2010. Web. 24 Oct. 2015.

"Where Does Lottery Revenue Go?" *ABC News.* ABC News Network, n.d. Web. 24 Oct. 2015.

JOINING THE MILITARY

Codevilla, Angelo M. "Tools of Statecraft: Diplomacy and War." *Foreign Policy Research Institute.* N.p., Jan. 2008. Web. 24 Oct. 2015.

Dart, Tom. "American Sniper Killer Eddie Ray Routh Found Guilty and Sentenced to Life in Prison without Parole." Guardian News and Media Ltd, 25 Feb. 2015. Web. 25 Oct. 2015.

Howell, Kellan. "Former Ranger Breaks Silence on Pat Tillman Death: I May Have Killed Him." *Washington Times.* The Washington Times, 19 Apr. 2014. Web. 25 Oct. 2015.

Hiller, Steven. "5 Myths About the Military You Believe (Thanks to Movies)." *Cracked.com.* Demand Media, Inc., 19 Feb. 2011. Web. 24 Oct. 2015.

Hsia, Tim, and Anna Ivey. "What the Army Doesn't Teach You." *Service to School.* N.p., 16 Jan. 2012. Web. 24 Oct. 2015.

"How to Be a Sonar Technician - Submarine | USNavy.com." *USNavycom.* N.p., 19 Aug. 2010. Web. 24 Oct. 2015.

"Living." *Today's Military.* U.S. Government, n.d. Web. 24 Oct. 2015.

Lucas, James A. "Study: U.S. Regime Has Killed 20-30 Million People since World War Two -- Sott.net." *SOTT.net.* CounterCurrents.org, 24 Apr. 2007. Web. 24 Oct. 2015.

Prager, Dennis. "Yes, We Are the World's Policeman." *National Review Online.* N.p., 17 Sept. 2013. Web. 24 Oct. 2015.

Stephens, Bret. "Off Duty as the World's Policeman." *US News & World Report.* N.p., 11 Dec. 2014. Web. 15 Oct. 2015.

"What Really Happened to Pat Tillman?" Ed. Kyra Darnton. N.p., 1 May 2008. Web.

MOST IMPORTANT MILLENNIAL

McGirt, Ellen. "Facebook's Mark Zuckerberg: Hacker. Dropout. CEO." *Fast Company.* Mansueto Ventures, 01 May 2007. Web. 24 Oct. 2015.

Rusli, Evelyn M. "The Education of Mark Zuckerberg." *The New York Times.* The New York Times, 12 May 2012. Web. 24 Oct. 2015.

Yadav, Sid. "Facebook - The Complete Biography." *Mashable*. Ed. Peter Cashmore. N.p., 25 Aug. 2006. Web. 24 Oct. 2015.

Erlewine, Stephen Thomas. "Lady Gaga." *Billboard.com*. N.p., n.d. Web. 24 Oct. 2015.

"Lady Gaga." *PEOPLE.com*. Ed. Julia Wang. Time, Inc., n.d. Web. 24 Oct. 2015.

"Lady Gaga Biography." Rolling Stone, n.d. Web.

Alter, Charlotte. "Malala Yousafzai: A Brief History of the Peace Prize Winner's Life." *Time*. Time, 9 Oct. 2014. Web. 24 Oct. 2015.

"Malala's Story." *World's Children's Prize - Malala's Story*. World's Children's Prize Foundation, n.d. Web. 24 Oct. 2015.

"Profile: Malala Yousafzai - *BBC News*." BBC News. N.p., 10 Dec. 2014. Web. 24 Oct. 2015.

Nussbaum, Greg. "Lebron James Biography for Kids." *Mr. Nussbaum*. Nussbaum Educational Network, n.d. Web. 24 Oct. 2015.

Silverman, Robert. "LeBron James Is a Better Leader than Michael Jordan Ever Was." *The Daily Beast*. Newsweek/Daily Beast, 5 May 2014. Web. 24 Oct. 2015.

Stewart, Mark, and Mike Kennedy. "JockBio: LeBron James Biography." *JockBio: LeBron James Biography*. BlackBook Partners, n.d. Web. 24 Oct. 2015.

GREATEST INVENTION OF MODERN TIMES

Cox, John Woodrow. "The History of the Mobile Phone." *Washington Post*. The Washington Post, 9 Sept. 2014. Web. 25 Oct. 2015.

Goodwin, Richard. "The History of Mobile Phones From 1973 To 2008: The Handsets That Made It ALL Happen." *Know Your Mobile*. Dennis Publishing, Ltd, 16 Apr. 2015. Web. 25 Oct. 2015.

Ray, Amanda. "The History and Evolution of Cell Phones." *The Art Institutes Blog*. N.p., n.d. Web. 25 Oct. 2015.

Dowling, Stephen. "World's Worst Planes." *BBC Future*. BBC, 22 May 2014. Web. 25 Oct. 2015.

Dwyer, Larry. "The Aviation History Online Museum." *The Aviation History Online Museum*. N.p., 1 June 2015. Web. 25 Oct. 2015.

Hallion, Richard P. "Airplanes That Transformed Aviation." *Air & Space Magazine*. Smithsonian Institution, July 2008. Web. 25 Oct. 2015.

Bellis, Mary. "History of Antibiotics." *About.com Inventors*. About.com, n.d. Web. 24 Oct. 2015.

Markel, Howard. "The Real Story Behind Penicillin." *PBS*. PBS, 27 Sept. 2013. Web. 24 Oct. 2015.

"Penicillin History." *MedicineNet*. WebMD, Inc., n.d. Web. 24 Oct. 2015.

Ang, Sarah. "14 Robotics Breakthroughs From the Past Decade." *Mashable*. N.p., 23 Oct. 2014. Web. 24 Oct. 2015.

Skitterbot.com. "Grey Walter's Tortoises." *YouTube*. YouTube, n.d. Web. 24 Oct. 2015.

Smith, Rene. "History of Robotics - Timeline, AI, Industrial, Toy Robots, Robotic Arm, Technology." *History of Robotics - Timeline, AI, Industrial, Toy Robots, Robotic Arm, Technology*. N.p., n.d. Web. 24 Oct. 2015.

Templeton, David. "Pitt Team Inserts Computer Chip in Brain so a Person's Thoughts Can Instigate Motion." *Pittsburgh Post-Gazette*. PG Publishing, Inc., 17 Dec. 2012. Web. 24 Oct. 2015.

TATTOOS FOR TEENS

Brennan, Lyle. "Still Starstruck: Young Belgian's Misery Three Years after She Had 56 Tattoos on Her Face." *Mail Online*. Associated Newspapers, 04 Feb. 2013. Web. 24 Oct. 2015.

Dechant, Lawrence. "Tattoo Removal Booms in Slow Job Market." *ABC News*. ABC News Network, 31 May 2012. Web. 24 Oct. 2015.

Emily, Intern. "13-Year-Old Scarred For Life After Getting Illegal Tattoo." *THE Q ROCKS*. N.p., 5 Nov. 2014. Web. 24 Oct. 2015.

Kennedy, Bruce. "In Tattoo Business, Profits Are Hardly Skin Deep." *Msnbc.com*. N.p., 15 Oct. 2010. Web. 24 Oct. 2015.

"100 Best Tattoo Quotes." *Tattoo Models Designs Quotes and Ideas*. N.p., 02 Apr. 2013. Web. 24 Oct. 2015.